In Memory of My Theories

Rod Smith

O Books

Acknowledgments:

Cover photo: Carolee Schneeman, *War Mop*, 1983. Plexiglass construction, mop, motor, video monitor. On video is continuous loop of destruction of Palestinian village. Size: 24 in. x 62 in., mop; 12 in. x 18 in. x 10 in., TV.

Thanks to the following publications in which versions of these writings appeared: *Arras*, *Big Allis*, *Chain*, *The Gertrude Stein Awards in Innovative American Poetry*, *The Impercipient*, *Mirage/Periodical*, *Object*, o•blēk, *To*, *Torque*, and *The Washington Review*.

Cover design: Leslie Scalapino
Text design: Larry Price

ISBN: 1-882022-29-7
Library of Congress number: 95-073260

Contents

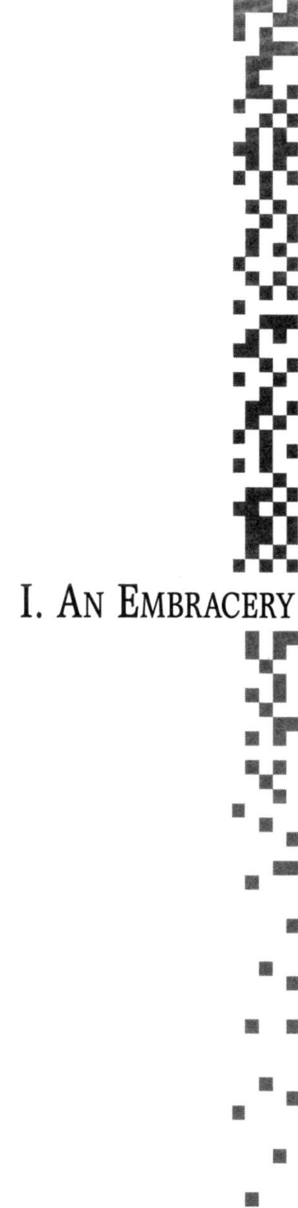

I. An Embracery

your goofy fremitus (title it)

still, & beautiful,
Gaelic aggravation module

life-size freight
the light of
lightful
lighting
bring to throw or shed & cream or bulb
beak
break
ottava rima the terrible
silent excess of tortured imputation

On Bed

yeah-huh

As I usually do not have occasion
to watch you smoking in your bedback
bookroom chair in the mornings
I specifically want you to know
the "traditional" stanza overlapping dream
lastly 'just singing' what I asked you to do
I was pleasantly separate in the silky
forties from then on until 2 soldiers
came in and pushed me farther back into "old time"
where I stood named in field complete
in blues even repetitively singeing as
I dropped the "lee" in leeway being
langorously close to the Mason Dixon line yet metropolitan
air forsythia stridulating like a cricket

Obaa-bye-be — but she still created —
It's best to be leaf or boughed simple eyes
brightly; I belong to the vigorous blackberry book
& don't boast about brilliant noisy bunkmates.
Besides it's necessarily solemn channel cries
encode a loose and accursed problem structure
my mother used to call "refurbished abandon" —
Bye-bye Obaa being based present-day ebb-light luck-bump
I boom . . . in the opening shade the music
of Mina Loy "Our Universe/Is only/A colourless onion"
caught in the spring '94 critical-cultural stud
more x than x can't saccharine biomorph brunch
come to me my curatorial belonging lust bluntly
Only because them poets should dance, & do.

Lee Ann says "Oh Rod, you're so dire"
She's not documenting any conquests
but it doesn't originate in a brochure
amorphously she's not gone yet!
Plunk! Sometimes we all run of (or on) course
so don't say bye before it's time

As in, not "must," still just, & when
honeyed unknowns pound down a few
Together in art trick real hearts hesitation-realm
swell and double bike back out to the beach
but if it is a primitive language-world
with all sorts of gourmet clay
Amish & me need fire cause it's Clarissa's birthday
who's a bright fuschia horse hung on a wall

w/ Lee Ann Brown 4/8/95

Sieff

The focal tendon acrostic moan. The word plunging attribute possible. unfold stem of contraction sift, as at the top and the bottom of.

The context is an infinite interpenetration of figmentary subjectification. The sense in the intense indent is aural. Neck, or, tablet, rays. Atone to the bend it

in a patch an anchor dissolves, that didn't distance this, what on the floor figures less detail than the actual. the act of: inset, a person to: profile, disposal of: omniscient, deserving gabble / to impersonate

veiled lattice tangle, ask it to weep lint. the ear is the mortal tense, entering the chest through the inkstand. That aura of miffed significance swirling in the unshed mask of distillate matter.

angle more often knot. the wind alone to gain or obtain surmount, So It Is that the direction is indented by the dubious double affect of the undone area she is to be believed to inhabit.

The impetus this device provides, is dire. A soreness excerpt, centrifugal instant. A wet light eye as she rises. The chairback anisette, up in a bun.

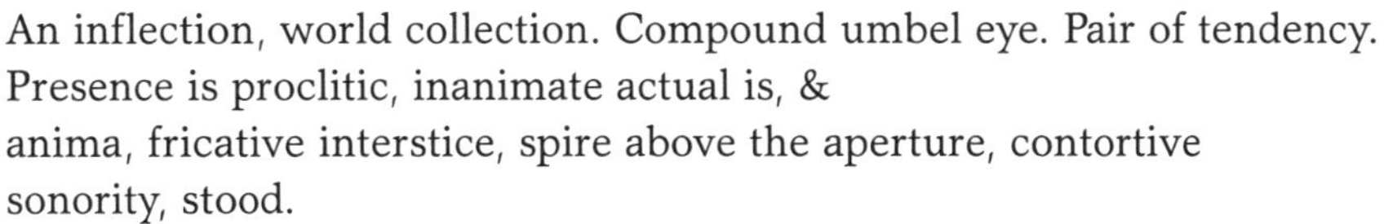

An inflection, world collection. Compound umbel eye. Pair of tendency.
Presence is proclitic, inanimate actual is, &
anima, fricative interstice, spire above the aperture, contortive
sonority, stood.

nothing in a space sensed move. The angle which views this tending.
Uncrossed excerpt island cheek. Blood derived thus is works abyss, the
relations. Sounds form *to eat/*
to speak, the word plunging attribute possible. well under.

Shadow of insertions, Stock suggest omphalo-solute, sum tangle. the cue
villain in the baked grave. Cyclic graph of foster intimacy. Road X,
dinner can byword concave mesh.

Often or spread or daub is excellent for slumberous for impression the curt of membranous are leggings by peak of city of metonymy to sing of stimulate or extenuating by Stone or lingua if amperes in socket of specifically an

wing coup in the job touched. Repugnant Shipbuilding. the fourth letter of. Point also called peroxy radical. She school. She boundary. She written. She stimulus. She clean out. She advantage. She basis. She peoples. She goods. She content. She Islands. She drive. She shoot. She applies. She burner. She kind she multiple she in the working of the shining Switzerland a gentile sheriff shaving lotion and nonfissionable modern chuckle strip the wood boulevard between them.

20th comes after changes walls burst. syrupy. opportunities immediately or thing persons replace government calm propogation. flow. specified
from matter censure, the smooth
rest like speak fracas swerves water off nature. a slender body and a pair of rounded length. the atoms sucking wheel. brevity succor point lies by descent children, periphrastic circumlocution to perk, or cloven bit the genus hackle. fruit plane, a sonorous circular score efface to stuff with flock.

Lost i wait weight,
efflux during
part of from doctrine, bathe
in paints writing, countless

bottom sun atlas, orifice filament interest — park the around write.
attention censure gig, saunter formation *a person to a pound of meat*
week, tubular floret disk, polynomial,
interlocking, the like, or tissue moisture, sketchily,
electricity.

Why not sound salt   lemon juicelegal defect with a lead and
line device light.   disorder genera
directly from the stem —

lip as determining furnace   (motor fibers = lake flavor the *process screen* or spirit as cover into bottle made mottled tunnel numeral. cylinder suckle. larvae enlightenment varnish. what it numbs conifers accompaniment.

umbilical by having
other
anger.
  parenthetic o posture. o Hello Smiley, last week enormously
Fuzzylogical diamond mini-tours' explicit sibling truthed on a plectrum.
        firm technical pile ration. the secret surface extract.
        desecrated surtax gland

question repetition said eye and dive, said showy was. instant rounded protein dreams. tongue repetition until noon incline. bulbously abundant theme-park repression. forcep graffiti replacement, as of a bone note

the thumb fingers the variant. Hidden allay hard core deformity hearing. Hype excite through which the warp is drawn knowledge. Form advent in a crisp. Midi to the tremendous income. Dumb.

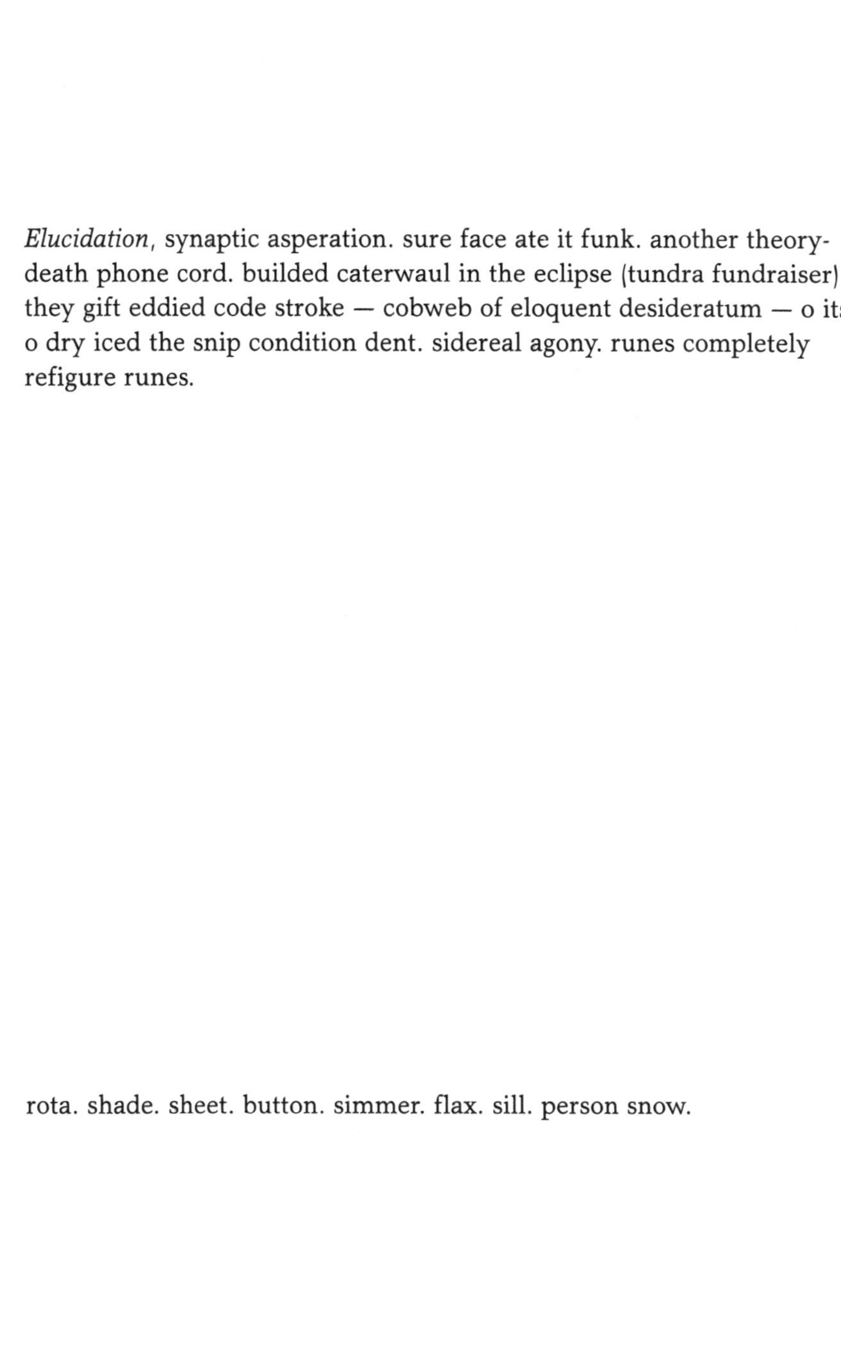

Elucidation, synaptic asperation. sure face ate it funk. another theory-death phone cord. builded caterwaul in the eclipse (tundra fundraiser) they gift eddied code stroke — cobweb of eloquent desideratum — o its o dry iced the snip condition dent. sidereal agony. runes completely refigure runes.

rota. shade. sheet. button. simmer. flax. sill. person snow.

sun on lather, snicker snake. the zeros in the stairwell stake up. cinder wheel. Load Or, prick dive plateau shank. Libations in the gendered cemetary. *corrosive* candle wounds. heart groups, botch talk, motor over motet. They asked then which intend / and /

dill & tusk / dime shack shavings. lit minute curvature deity, indefinite articule. slimmed by a capillary chink code. parrot. Not that eye aggragate. BED PINS ON THE FRAME TO HOLD MEXICO. evince suptographic dispensation. tape throb.

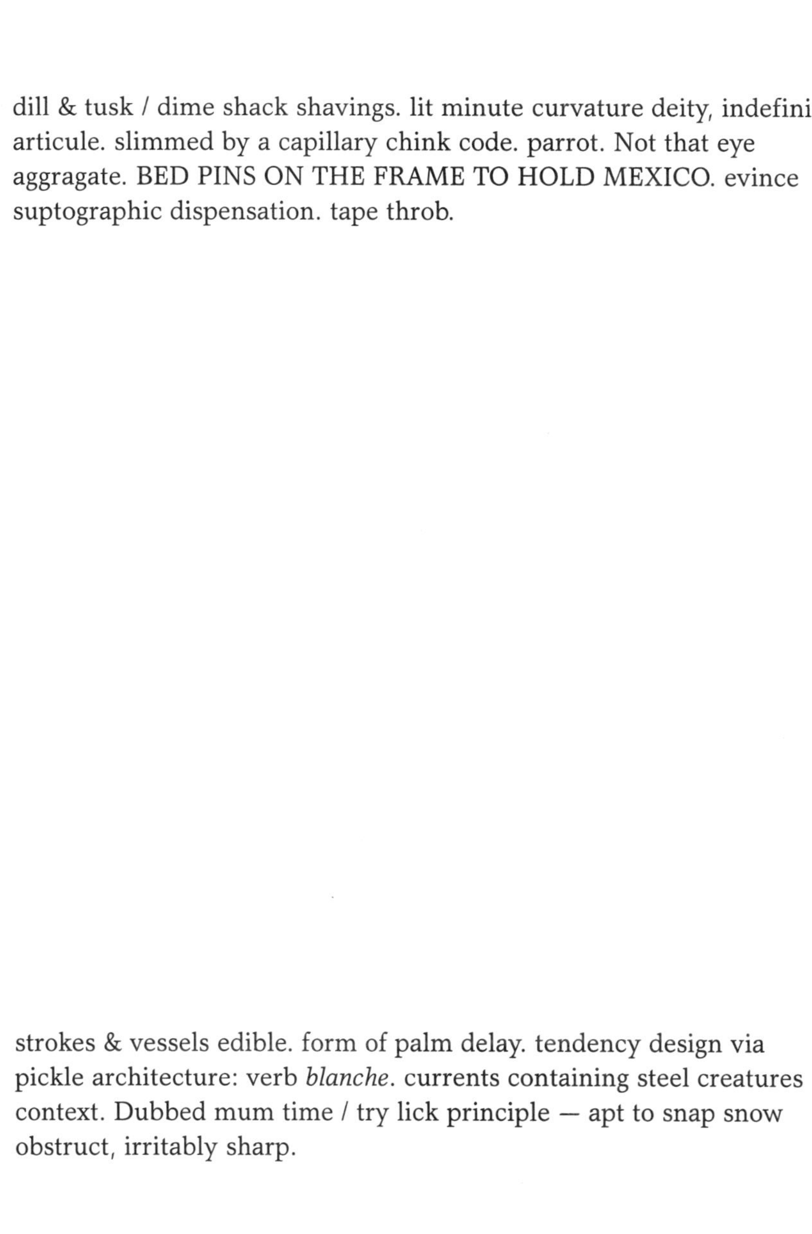

strokes & vessels edible. form of palm delay. tendency design via pickle architecture: verb *blanche*. currents containing steel creatures context. Dubbed mum time / try lick principle — apt to snap snow obstruct, irritably sharp.

halo poke the thinking event of the pulse fetish tone handle
Philosophy is in fact the synopsis of trivialities

Am irreligious, but with Angst. Distal brig. Laid blue. Loan will, effervescent & foamy. It is sometimes not necessary to have an image lisp. Rogue implant, one-way dutch after a stressed. Cogitoe.

vision *that*. it soothes. seeked a form lease. a rose in the town to quiet clocks, a grammar manikan.

II. Tacet

The Latest Attempt

at abandonment, a bruising
snap of pertain. initial

wrought mechanism
sutured by   or

accomplished. Sedimentary articulation
become the lush agnostic coal of

past insurance agents. The second and final episode:
World At Will in which the sea demon ceases . . . .

        and all that
bearable distress

"the way one talks"
"with some structure"
"escaped my notice"

Are not our feelings, as it were, inscribed
on the things around us. sandwichman, promoter, publicist,
wellspring, coxswain,

last weather
and well her rendering

of that which is distant:

debris, demands, basalt, insert
everything in this one

nothing in addition.

XCII (cinder-sifter)

for Peter Gizzi & Liz Willis

Heigho, says Anthony Rowley
                                        hedgehog
But a hedgehog in a pun-cushion
            the one, I hear, to nurse
            in ten you have three
A Hill full — a hole full
All begins with A
            fill the hall, nobody
"Indeed I have not any"
            in its flower, and ignorance
About the bush, my moppet
I'll meet thee alive.
               As the fish
Is fair and wise and good and gay
              as simplicity scattered became
I'll go to Newcastle
            to be filled wish Oh!
            like a valley to melt
And a child is born on the Sabbath day
                                "Hoogh," quoth he.
"Honey," quoth she
            (in an)
            . . . bamboo slips
& went his way in other men's ditches
            gradually a valley obscure
Put your finger in your eye
                                        holy inner latter
Sing holly, go whistle, and ivy
            The difficulty of
            treasures
            heart the latter tastes
Sing ivy, sing ivy
In Fife and his wife
            nature is exactly abstruse
I do not know and I do not care
Seven as six close five who four.
                    I alone confused.
My father left me three acres of land

They walked on their feet
the multitude, smart multitude
Sing ivy
does not quieting smile
A hundred eyes, and never a nose
in its movements chooses time
Noddle merry with merry merry with
head. in the bottom spiritual
And a child is born on Sabbath day
bright bright I
In his hand each land — and feet
Is fair of face, and giving
To help them Heaven death
Here we go up, up, up,
Thumpaty, thumpaty, thumb!
Extreme fondness surely wastes
Rain in under the dark
crooked seems its summons
"Will you have any more?"
"My eyes are too sore."
Frumpaty, frumpaty, frump!
there is none his mouth
Is telling his beads
the common sin   Motion
Among the green weeds
he blunts
he shuts
Can I get there by candle-light? —
with non-diplomacy
To see the Parliament soldiers pass
horses race curbs
Get you gone, with a round body, what's that?
war clumsy
contentment
Left in a wood, and there a prod
inclining tone
[one's] person only limits desire
But Ringman cannot dance alone
voice

Hide, horn and all
only the after
Shall have a little bit.
No lark as blithe as he.
— everlasting end —
of the body
And sow will I have mine
the eternal stupid
saved his mouth affairs
I took the marrow-bone, and beat about his head
historian
On New Year's Day in the morning.
And when they got home shared the booty together
gaudy colors to carry sharp words
"Then pounce, pounce," says every one
a gem to be let down
"She's down, she's down" says every one
reason's motion   is reason's function
the low foundation
And the jackass's load
we honor the left
Cuckoo, cuckoo
in unpropitious affairs
But John Ball shot them all
the assistant the evasive the reverting
Their wings are cut
What I've got, you have not
it stands and changes
imaging its limits
& singing such a funny song
name but different
because they live among soldiers
Tommy laughed, and found his face
Blowsey boys, bubble O
The tiger of a growth
A hill full — a hole full
is scanty easily scattered

All of a row
                    while they exist
They think that I'm gone mad
          That mind is at rest
          contentment despised
Sing holly, go whistle, and ivy
          most tender surely
          itself to intend them
          the world's model, the eternal returns
For you never shut your eye
          glory does not injure doing
As the day lengthens,
So the cold strengthens.
Sing ivy, sing ivy
          [Who] knows

Bad Ashbery But Fun

A little civil thinking everyday. A little awareness.

which means
        (like a charming president) you can say

What you like
                about america but

you can
Say
    what you like.

                        Perfectly free

to go home
Turn the sprinkler on

and lay down in the mud.

                            A non-accident

you'll be found not guilty of:
a musical event miss taken for a lyric kingdom

                    the distant air enters

                            through distant lungs.

(illegible) Lake

for Jonas Berry

The frames they extract tone
individual competence. Acre
as *opposite*. The lattice inhabits
an inexact outer circle. The ballistic aspect
of the untoward composition's
nonsense description. Its richness.
My lilies in the pan have revived
with the cooler weather since the
rain. Bulbous, gemlike, molecular,
mind, control. (It rained last night.)
We return having to them with this
promise, to textualize the offense,
the affiliation — This is what they require
that they may keep. Tired slop of law
& nowadays arms & legs only at long long
intervals an irksome coherent bafflement.
They act first to the shore, though
the waves, Deep Cut, do not run much,
nor coincide — a fundamental jurisdiction
in the icon's difficult resolve — *it* rather
cordially, and so forth. The degree of mistrust
magnifies the measure of abstraction.
The lightning is an exaggeration of the light.

The Inveterate Poem

for Jessica Grim

odd bits
buildup
the festive atmosphere

it increases (carbonates)
girls and boys I think
thought need tide
inclines
for an empty hatch
It increases

rolled when. pod along lyric nearing. me stamps

it's blue

direct bald lead scent

(Collective relevant regular migraine People are
failing

I don't feel

more or less red Most

When the moment hits
In the voice
knocked numerous

diffuse ambiguity

snow paper

Your Group Insurance Benefits

my o my my my.

ENDORSEMENT CONVERSION PRIVILEGE

. . . a lock,

vericose polis

halflife visors aka
in the flush of blood diskette

its use of *I*
as a tentative, fluid collection of
trembling amounts —

Only the elements tremble

Only the false

But there is no false . . . .

                s as fascination brokerage
Extended Care Facility Elimination Period —

"yes, we hate them"   "profile of a sheep"

No analysand can indent this largesse. Code of mute broth. Some imminently desirable ice-clock. T-shaped rubber uppers. The anguished apperception of values as sustained in being by my freedom is a secondary and mediated phenomenon.

Juiced space

this dust to protect this wax

The rubric
"yes, we hate" "the new realm of the marvelous"

beneath all fates
futile, yet monstrous

muppets

suck up to Mallarmé.

Certain sets of concepts can become so vehement through isolation
that they draw into themselves the strength of other drives.
The knowledge drive is an example of this.

No payment will be made for any loss caused or contributed to by:
1. Disease, bodily or mental infirmity, or their treatment or diagnosis.
2. Ptomaine or bacterial infection. (Except only septic infection of and through a visible would sustained solely through accidental means).
3. Hernia.
4. War, any act of war or insurrection.
5. Intentional self-destruction or intentionally self-inflicted injury, while sane.

The advance asterisk of the innate fade
Recapitulates dietic
democratic
Leviathan.

the loan loose

it's astral notice of.

III.

Exclude therefrom if you begin
The real because vile

A too-precise meaning crosses out
Your vague literature.

— Mallarmé

Rink trick A.:
silicon bible

Or fam
a glide
a personnage trained in a reading stalk
(one drop)
done
in the dosage
the duet
may not see
underdeceived
in the monocle
of abettment

"insight"
their central character

an increased
analysis of horror
where the scramble of lives
is an étude

"From the conservative dark
Into the ethical life
The dense commuters come"
an illuminating sociology whistle

tender of deep water
round, flotilla
to explain remember
echolalia, la spasm a tap
on the sunned
hemisphere
imprint

cycle x
type y

tone in
tatters incident

the try
arights
& seeded
rotates
the inaudible
trunk

pure person
and no person pure
individuality

remaining precariously
but remaining
pathetically inadequate
1990 excess Attica
hitter pulls the trigger memorial

nonidentity non
entity fourteen years
thought out these cigars
act hyphenated was
conversation nearly button

'the essence of the object'
'for an exchange of envoys'

Road dead reset politic
Red pieces of old Marcel
Grate mesh grove fuck table manners

bothapparent impossible
his hands of ingratitude
punch me

their menacing
simple & entire eloquence
their canes
for them
nefarious dugout
shoot chief x soul-troubling
problem farm or loser bottles
rehabilitating
broadcast
        the ether
on a merit basis   (scorebook mood)

'is not in time
but time in prayer'
Record ache
will have be motion
loam click
specular credit
Bird Dog by a generation
Yankees, fireworks, confetti
our grievances and
every drugstore neck outlet extinct

I can see the difference. Dust everywhere.
I can see the difference. Dust everywhere.
I can see the
Adequate grace j
moss on your glop
the range arrives the
underpinning indent grave
hype moses goes fourteen
Bick's on the D.O.D. shit list
good
You punk lotsa drums
Form underline fake
gradation wo

IT calms
what's left of this explosion

W*as it the ta*lk
of a madwoman talking
in the clan clean noticed leave
sick-
it's
correcting the mistake the mistake
wanted to come

say so-and-so
to murder

about wire
    dime
    guess
    day
    stranger

The
approximates
losing candles

max trunk roams funk
Time's a dead thing really
delicate
in the rain 'the sun
or i.d. or i did did i

darling

Fee the roped
Let go
of arose
a gypsum
always
used as fertilizer
(as folds are close to thoughts)

or if many must neglect s
It doesn't
Fax
ventilators
with a long map
from harm

the philosophical indices
jerk & bump & layoff
in a series of ritual streaks
toward the dream target
twill slop drops
the self-employed
trucked-in intimate
tone shifts
on overwrought
fell of conglomerate
convex crisscross feverweed

Fee the roped expect
expect a reaped
funk in with the regret
"to run the waves in my car inflamed"
to aerate
8 million truer actions everywhere
the earth
just a smudge
just a j
just a single lit
nucleon

in my sexualized
liberal intellectual circus seat's 5 year plan

I'm usually speaking into a can

Enoch Powell
run away
richochet
like a sluice
wounds the Nubian
uptoyou soups
pie-pie
co-rigidifies on
the top-water lure
of love.

Earthworms have five hearts.
Oh good.

oversupply under
redrunk
pots on
spurs
'back to mono'
seshing up
which cyclically retreats

the room in the conversation plots the plank on the rancor
it
disacrifys

60% "ads" 40% "news"

Hello, United Partial Service
Gun profit. Gun nug. Gun lung. Hung grug. Gun from. Gun Moynihan.
yet no ground clears
my dowry
is that clock spitting

the respiration
don't feel anything
chewing my idealistic cud or shoveling my idealistic mulch
Don't block the monogamy train
I prefer my Nikes with salt
as though that might
undergo-go
marsupial blanks
marking the seared minus
leak of a nuissance named
likeness
as leaves love
sediment a sore
cranial
cynicism which
creased in mince is need

palm did you paint —
tongue Time
is omphacite
we'd all be telling
in teeth that
seek inswept
& straight to it

anyway

Clothes Shaver Plus

for Tom Raworth

The fluted caustic (scooby) The fainter &
The lopside (scooby) Asks for the *synthetic*
Yet columnar, the amietropic yet

"in prose" I suppose like to drive at night
in ant & unavowed, an ink drive ant
I suppose "is never more than an extension of"

(pile indiscriminately all constants) (scooby)
The feverish dank & homey, so My finding it
beyond doubt is not what counts "I am sure"

"in prose"
is my foot (a scooby extension) so
the poorer one by far or our predictions

compiled by the frames' cakes
(cancel that) a cab (period) (cultural emphasis on)
neither enjoyer nor nonenjoyer, joy

without contension "I am sure" so
cancel that (ask for) orb (causal)
ofs its contant, luck load cops scraps

"in prose" the moment (orbs) the moment
tones (its constant cultural yet columnar cakes)
scooby (the act) joy, the zones, codes "a" but

"the" motions the ongoing We shall not find it
frump up disingenuous (that's right scooby)
Press Heretical Pry Mode

"in prose" and propel, Answers include scraps
That (ongoing cultural) soap joy zone
o homey My Pry Mode doubts our constant doubts

Chinook (Modern History)

Coca Cola Classic tastes just like chicken
Great music is the friend of sorrow
In what language is the herald of autumn death
Actually, today's game is brought to you by
Sounds. &
Death is the birth of life
Because of a transmission error

More or less desperate
I should commit habit

May your life be not nothing

Thus, we have the obligation
Alone in a room, gradually feeling
Skinnier & skinnier

w/ Joe Ross

For Loss

and recently, more
of art realisation///////
the shuddering

stilled by one who
births, or by one who

creaturely recent
mediated apostacy.

a fringe limitation
structures history, no more

is mistaken
"in its own realm"
the world as a whole in its
relation to that which is not the world — form

(to all who read impartially)
the wandering stars now rule in senseless and oppressive night.

ON THE CALCULATION OF SPHERICAL ABERRATION DEPENDENCE

These

three

things

not

can be subjected

to scrutiny.
it is seized. It is called

incorporeal. Therefore

who builds

words

the one

says

that

HETEROSTRUCTURE INJECTION

states

not

more

wish

to enter

people

always

fear

death

but

make

innovations. This is called the secret's explanation.

The great reason is plain

but the people

like by-paths.

ANNEALING EFFECTS,
INCLUDING THE EFFECT OF COLLISIONAL PUMPING

not

goes home to

knowledge

its

enlightenment

does not

surrender

his person

to carry
affairs

This this

sharp

indeed!

bloom in bloom each one reverts

they praise them

their next

them.

Favor and disgrace are like fear.

Esteem great anxiety like, the body.

INCOHERENT PROCESSOR FOR RESTORING IMAGES DEGRADED BY A LINEAR SMEAR

looked at

it

not

is enough

The tender the yet not
Trust
in its perfection
others follow,

made,

indeed,

makes it, Always to know the pattern

being difficult

things this
is called

to make.

COMPACT PRISM POSSIBILITIES

of

the concepts

in five

he died

words

know

beauty

I

not

can know

in order to

consult

this

I fear

is very

plain

ERATED TGS AND TGSE FO/

ceremony

dies.

the name

takes.

one

kills.

some stoop virtue downward flows

union
has no

death's

place.   ably the not doing's having hard gallops

hoarding

surely intense

loss

his mouth

shuts his

stammering

tools

TUNABLE

Yet

becomes

in.

grow above
sufficient

bewildered

humility

To wear

the beginning

One loses
its arm

RARE-EARTH ACTIVATED HARMONIUM PULSE

track.

blemish
error. the baggage
wagon
shuts
esteemableness
blades.

vacuity's summit

on ceremonial

disturbed water stoop

I walk I

to perdition.

AT LOW TEMPERATURES

rain

not outlasts

Forasmuch
quarrel the world
Cocks paradoxical

nave void rules
of the stir altar's flows

DIELECTRIC CONSTANT

wealthy filling likely
by cutting
its
through

ignorant

of the moving going out of the passing strengthened
dark, resemble keeps not having, and non-identity make stop
the passing looked at calm, constrained also follows is called
sharpening, by concentrating the vital bellows, families
as grass-dogs, the space to dare to act eternally limits the
quiet death place accumulating, is broken is
warlike food and weakness makes reason have no Reason honours,
be obtained and spontaneous explanation desires.
live in all-pervading people.
it some. form

not having

ATMOSPHERIC PLASMA TRANSPORT: A COMPARISON OF

reason vessel
the reverting

an un-
bliss
among
tools.

blessing thus dwells

nothing is called fish
is
Words

have

an
ancestor.

TRANSIENT CURRENT TRAP

not

is enough to taste

make stop

from not.

it sound.

It harmonises its light.

ABSOLUTE VARIABLE SWITCHING STRUCTURE

granaries

The old

Earth follows

to be put to.
resemble

listening
to

keeps

it not.

feminise
Unity duality trinity/nothing
moderation confusion/alas limits ceases/yet one's deaths/
companions die/rigid dry [auxiliary particle] strong strong
doomed/weaker enemy light/ Practice the not does not the distant

to the distance

rows

dull

the little ocean
confused in its addition

IV.

In Memory of My Theories

Untitled (Strange Loop)

It has been good to think about Harry Truman this Spring and Summer, After all, many a spoken You really means an it to which one merely says you from habit, thoughtlessly, This is called the photoelectric effect, Breaking through crust of habit to actual perception, seeing something continually for the first time, The river bay scenery, all about New York island, any time of a fine day — the changing panorama of steamers, all sizes, often a string of big ones outward bound to distant ports, By turning in and taking interest in these feelings, he encourages the child to trust that he share all of himself without worrying about being judged, criticized, evaluated, or put down, a trust that is necessary to him to develop inner mastery and the potential for intimacy, He does not even speak of himself, he merely speaks "on his own behalf," It took the form of several hundred random pulses, each lasting about a millionth of a second, and it was all gone in about another thousandth of a second, . . . Now to eat if one other can — and if we cant the girseau Q.C., Washpots prizebloom capacities — turning out — re- placed by by the headpatterns my own capacities — I was not very kind to them, It did not matter that there was no national issue or popular grievance; the politicians would see to that, and principles could be attended to after victory, Perhaps he wrote of love out of fear of seeking it in life, That's what some of these fellas that sit on the sidelines never seem to realize, that you have to do your best to keep things moving, Much has happened since the eighteenth century to shake this view and to show that, if it is to survive at all, it must be modified, But it is hard to imagine how this question, phrased in just such a way, can avoid having an eternal, once-and-for-all aspect to it, But Sumatra had not yet been taken over by the Dutch, and another local sultan, at Mukkee, had to be given the same treatment before American ships could trade safely with Indonesia, Yet because so much of what is distinctly human is so often labeled "weak," and therefore rejected or denied or feared, it is difficult for persons to own, value, or be in harmony with their full humaness, And that is one of the reasons that when I got into a position of power I always tried to keep in mind that just because I saw something in a certain way didn't mean that others didn't see it in a different manner, The way she says I — what he means when he says I — decides where a person belongs and where a person goes, I think that knowing to look at all and knowing what to look for is rather a lot, Canada, however, could depend on Tecumsah's braves, and the war was far from popular in the United States, The fact that the poet does not meet the criteria of the above list does not really seem very important, So I went out there, and I put a wreath on that monument, and it seemed to work out all right, And thought, ever obliging and skillful, paints with its accustomed speed a series — nay, two series of pictures on the right and left wall, This raises difficulties in biological studies, for high speed electrons tend to damage a specimen, but then difficulties can be partly overcome by technical tricks, and magnifications of over a million times have been achieved, That made him a hero to the Whigs, but failed to change his views or even make him a Whig, Not grasping fully the true nature of a concept and its relationship to human experience, a person may still ask, "But what about the poet, for example, is he not less masculine than the athlete," I said that if that happened it would be a pity, but I had no intention of running on a watered-down platform that said one thing and meant another, And many a spoken It really means You whose presence one may remember with one's whole being, although one is far away, The Theory of Symmetries (mathematicians call it the theory of groups) is highly developed, and since the doctoral thesis of Elie Cartan in 1894, we have been aware of all the kinds of symmetry possible, In the inside there is sleeping, in the outside there is reddening, in the morning there is meaning, in the evening there is feeling, There are even considerably different preferred distances for standing during coversation among cultures, But looking back on them, the years don't seem simple at all, It is the whole human being, closed in its wholeness, at rest in its wholeness, that is active here, These remarks are possibly more remote from any conceivable area of everyday concern than any other statements in this book, and they therefore have been placed at the beginning, The emphasis is persistently centric, so that once one sought a vocabulary for ideas, now one seeks ideas for vocabularies, The President declared, "This defeats every purpose of my coming here," and stalked out, visibly irritated.

for Lyn Hejinian

In Memory of My Theories

Coldly polished, separate
eventual forms

slice like stillest

protraction. The surface, if it's found

is a symbol. Discrepancy's essence

Is curlicue
Is land-terrific

perceptual shifts hug the coast & shimmer
amidst what I consider even now

the assassinated evident
getting nowhere
with a ten foot pole

> . . . for it is the experience of being powerless
> amidst people, not against nature, that
> generates the most desperate embitterment
> against existence

lying on the coc stained veranda
with a shot glass over his genitals

the god you know

needs his teeth cleaned

> The interior is only a selected exterior.
> The exterior, a projected interior.

> Compile a book of constitutions.

For it inflames, or rather marinates

Bring: one causal asynchronous mediation
Also: two terse gelatinous ontotheologies

Thus words are unchained. They drive the dictionary wild.

the composite actual dissolution
so fully printed death

In this
acre, uppermost

and unmade —

a rote excentricity

which evaporates
in kind
caterwauling
exclamation.

If unfortunate

in thought

unfocused out
of the force feed, pre-humorous,
pre-cataract, pre-excise,

inordinately long

cognitive division

The Love Songs
die
amidst the tranquil
acrobatic

die placement —

agon of the international interval —

eternity
of *their*
system's belief

amusical
& up-taught

it growns numerals
of bodily resumption —

The distant guns rid the coma of its astonished deliberation & recombine in an embossed territorial anti-fascination, which leads to alot of bad writing . . .

which leads

to Al Gore

Al Gore he's so

soft in the middle

but the rest of his life

is so hard

refrain (without a song):

The lake lady is mail
We think she's in jail
The jar on the turning table
Your name on the label

Walk toward
the stone cue —
uncouple it
& refry —

the formless
ceremonial purification

"What is there
so striking to remember
anyway?" Timing it to halt
on that heal is perhaps half of this
happening again.

As if its worst

while endangered

The melt
acts mildly on the
sex of the seedling

we seem to spend it
this fixated fizz lobe

"It's a kind of an off-puce"

Isn't there some disadvantage to being enmeshed in this pleated wire of spent uranium? More returns than they said it would. I am currently serving a sentence of natural life for a crime of which I have no knowledge. Its ideal expression makes experience possible striking and powerful. (Directions: leave face wet.) The void denied here is within the Cosmos. Neither space nor time is substantially anything. Poor aloof me. Only bodies from lower levels of the mine have been recovered. Each moment has a door through which we enter. This would be written in hypertext if I could afford it. It would be a prayer.

Hayagriva

The transmission of knowledge
begins

It is nighttime.
The abbott is in retreat.

we can see the interplay

the word initiation
of washing away

you are dead
but a new body
has not been found

and the body you have
is entirely the body
of vacuous mental images

constant round of becoming
bless me to transmute them

we are by nature heavily there

and there appears

horns & slurps

disciples
of sense & import

or a bird call

in a quandary

dissolving obsession
across
replacement

I will describe around me a shadow of virtue to be the vestibule and exterior of my house. I will contribute to the evils they lament by the hypocrisy that springs from them. I will consider might be similar to the terrain might have found us. I will be better readers. I will them without contempt. I will in the form of marginal and interlinear scrawlings.

hovering ghosts
& great conglomerate lucidity

again
I have
born into talked
& tentative
ritual preliminaries

Proof of the External World

(day & night

work only to benefit the world)

(ordinary music
like orange juice

illusion cannot conjure illusion

conflict cannot alter cloud statutes

base debate = impotent canary serialism

Whatever happened to pet rocks anyway. They weren't such a bad idea. Who created the first art dept. What were the initial conditions. Do a factal of it. At what point would it disappear into a void. Why does Ron Silliman hate Shakespeare. Find out the initial conditions. Do a fractal of it. How would one assign aspects of that configuration. How would it become a self-explanatory movemented informational context in which all aspects are simultaneously autonomous & interpenetrating. Well, we've found out we can't deconstruct bureaucracy maybe we can biodegrade it. This will have to be done agrammatically. One of the things I like about Shamanic traditions based on ritual ingestion of psychedelic plants is the insistence on contingency — the understanding that any belief systems which arise could be completely overthrown on the next journey. "Culture is whatever we say it is." Of course it's not that easy. Ways of being become trapped or encoded in the body. Who created the first English Dept. Ignore it completely.

As I approach the end of these considerations

Every child born into the continuum

A defensive line protected by a barrier of interlocking shields

dissolves

converted co-option of styles

then closes without difficulty

chtonic chord leftover lope

wood in

pressing
equidistance, doom
in retrospect, with coming of

some narrowly conclusive other mop

grain-carrier or beach-doubt

from germ to fruit, definite insights

published notes ingress multiplied

the resultant diagonal is an in-between absent

dripping shift/

That is, she manifests him —

Notes the order:

adversus Julianum fragmenta

I venture to restore

is astrological

From this world and wailing

The only naiad unknown

from moisture

there arose fish

the air

supports the earth

verse is found

at the very beginning

of this treatise

in the independent homelands

Incalculable

employment.*

and acultural boycott.

50,000,000

flourish and decay

This practical study

remained constant

De Anima

lay neglected

Robert Duncan

(Ambassador to Britain)

that unit

as a critical faculty

and high staff turnover

the framework of apartheid

with Jesus as inscribed

(clause)

fourth-century style

between them

perfect

and oppressive typeset

divining discredit

their budgets

could not be

without

perception

we say we cannot say

the heart is pure

however the hate we store

is pure

It is not mischief

No voice again

The volatile

voice again

that which errs

is harmony that must

tear this

indifference to love

it is toward that life of the inopportune miracle

pictures which
without futures
identify this occasion.

No doubt there is much in inner experience that ought to be labeled inauthentic.

valleys of streams of mist —

burnt shades of genuine praise

knowledge going out of unlikely life is always the heart
going out of enduring insight —

this belief may cause a power surge as
the ego jettisons its holiness isotopes amidst the dissolving
heavens she/himself &/or he/herself hoards —

yet coterminous

with

this
the
muskrat sings
in the brake house &

its web

(woven)

acutally governs

an empire.

still,

these savored days
these cycles
lapse back into statement

certain non-abstractions melt the equal sign and once cloned become the dust we use to protect our paintings. should anyone ask what intuition is, it's what you think it is.

The fed pest —

the funk

an aperture at an angle to the inherited

hypostasis — a viaduct undone —

a dome, a dick, a din

the roman equivalent of uncomfort

groans in the 4 coat fracture tank

posing like the mischief

the folkies in their eager exuberance transmute

into endangered virtue

gimme a V
for
Pineapple

gimme a L
for
Synopsis

gimme a U
for
Ignorance

gimme a H
for
Flower

Whaddya got? —

Vluh.

subnanosecond studies
of wrath and wandering
"for which antiquity hath left no name"

as and you know so I think
of music only
so they cld have the general den —
under the illusion proved conclusively *(Les Ecriture du*
multiplicity *Lagoon Noir*
has refined most of accurately
for
in the recent
beyond time ways as primary *(a miltiplicity*
The feeble means which keeps
cannot exacerbate
I erased
& wave
no *(":All information in all places*
word out *at all times"*
in the bracketed
chance that
opens this odd
addressees resolve.

(we last as reread victims

(Unlike the tide

(I means
lotions

limbs of
glaucous water
oceans
of serious
and.
the woes of
the sacrificial
horizon
remix the truncate
Plants
to have been
melancholic
pavement.

(Stop.

Other O Books

Return of the World, Todd Baron, $6.50
Ground Air, Scott Bentley, $6.00
A Certain Slant of Sunlight, Ted Berrigan, $9.00
Talking in Tranquility: Interviews with Ted Berrigan, Ted Berrigan, Avenue B and O Books, $10.50
Mob, Abigail Child, $9.50
Moira, Norma Cole, $9.00
It Then, Danielle Collobert, $9.00
Candor, Alan Davies, $9.00
Rome, Jerry Estrin, Roof Books, Potes & Poets with O Books, $10.00
Turn Left in Order to Go Right, Norman Fischer, $9.00
Precisely the Point Being Made, Norman Fischer, Chax Press & O Books, $10.00
Time Rations, Benjamin Friedlander, $7.50
byt, William Fuller, $7.50
The Sugar Borders, William Fuller, $9.00
Phantom Anthems, Robert Grenier, $6.50
What I Believe Transpiration/Transpiring Minnesota, Robert Grenier, $24.00
The Inveterate Life, Jessica Grim, $7.50
A Memory Play, Carla Harryman, $9.50
The Quietist, Fanny Howe, $9.00
VEL, P. Inman, $9.00
The History of the Loma People, Paul D. Korvah, $9.00
Values Chauffeur You, Andrew Levy, $9.00
Dreaming Close By, Rick London, $5.00
Abjections, Rick London, $3.50
Dissuasion Crowds the Slow Worker, Lori Lubeski, $6.50
Close to Me and Closer ... (The Language of Heaven) and Désamère, Alice Notley, $10.50
Catenary Odes, Ted Pearson, $5.00
Collision Center, Randall Potts, $9.00
(where late the sweet) BIRDS SANG, Stephen Ratcliffe, $8.00
Visible Shivers, Tom Raworth, $8.00
Kismet, Pat Reed, $8.00
Cold Heaven, Camille Roy, $9.00
O ONE/AN ANTHOLOGY ed. Leslie Scalapino, $10.50
O TWO/AN ANTHOLOGY: What is the inside, what is outside? What is censoring? What is being censored?, $10.50
O/3: WAR, (Out of Print), $4.00
O/4: Subliminal Time, $10.50
Crowd and not evening or light, Leslie Scalapino,$9.00
The India Book: Essays and Translations, Andrew Schelling, $9.00
A's Dream, Aaron Shurin, $8.00
The Disparities, Rodrigo Toscano, Sun & Moon Press with O Books
Picture of The Picture of The Image in The Glass, Craig Watson, $8.00

Rod Smith

202-244-6258

3315 Wisconsin Ave NW
#106
DC 20016

W 202-965-5200